Advice
from a
Mountain

20 🌾 16
Better World Press, Inc.
Oregon   Colorado   New Mexico

Published by Better World Press, Inc.
A Division of Your True Nature, Inc.
P.O. Box 272309, Fort Collins, Colorado 80527
800-992-4769 email: branch@yourtruenature.com
yourtruenature.com

Silk painting cover and tree Illustrations: Ilan Shamir
Mountain woodcut illustrations: Chuck Black
Library of Congress Cataloging-in-Publication Data
ISBN 978-1-930175-34-1
  Shamir, Ilan, 1951-
        Advice from a Mountain / Ilan Shamir
        1. Mountains
        2. Human Growth and Potential
        3. Nature
        4. Health and Wellness

Printed in the USA on recycled paper. Many thanks to
the trees for their gift of paper! All paper used in the printing of this
book has been replanted through the 100% Replanted program.
Visit www.ReplantTrees.org

Let your words be uplifting and strong. Rise above any doubts or limitations that keep you from living each day with joy. Leave no stone unturned as the mountain shares its timely wisdom to help you stand in strength and live your true nature.

The mountains, the rivers, the wildflowers, and the cloud patterns calm me in the midst of yet another busy day. I find patience and support from the mountain's song, and I stand with renewed serenity.

There are days when I feel on loose ground, not sure of where I stand and not firm about who I am. The tall mountains, which have been anchored in the earth and reaching to the sky for millions of years, help me return to solid ground.

We all need useful advice to guide us in living a good life. Here, the mountain encourages us to reach high and rock our world. As John Muir so beautifully wrote, "The mountains are calling and I must go."

Advice from a
Mountain...

Dear Friend . . .

Reach New Heights

Savor Life's Peak Experiences

There Is Beauty as Far as the Eye Can See

Stand in the Strength of Your True Nature

Be Uplifting

Follow
the
Trails
of the
Wise
Ones

Protect and
Preserve
Timeless
Beauty:

Silence

Solitude

Serenity

Flowing Rivers

Ancient Trees

Rise Above
It All

Make Solid
Decisions

Climb Beyond
Your Limitations

Leave No
Stone
Unturned

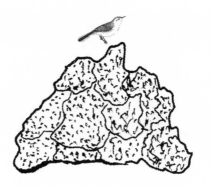

Never Take Life
for Granite

Get to
the Point

Have Patience,
Patience,
Patience

Take Life's Ups and Downs in Stride

Let Your Troubles Vanish into Thin Air

To Summit
All Up . . .

Enjoy the Journey

Step by Step

By Step

Rock On!

Advice
from a
Mountain

Dear Friend . . .

Reach new heights

Savor life's peak experiences

There is beauty as far as the
eye can see

Stand in the strength of
your true nature

Be uplifting

Follow the trails of the Wise Ones

Protect and preserve timeless beauty:
    Silence
    Solitude
    Serenity
    Flowing rivers
    Ancient trees

Rise above it all

Make solid decisions

Climb beyond your limitations

Leave no stone unturned

Never take life for granite

Get to the point

Have patience, patience, patience

Take life's ups and downs in stride

Let your troubles vanish into thin air

To summit all up . . .
Enjoy the journey
        Step by step
        By step

Rock on!

Caring for
the Earth

Standing, looking at the mountain before me, I appreciate that it makes me feel small. The mountain speaks of the vastness of nature. It inspires me to be mindful of the natural world and to show my gratitude by becoming a steward of the earth. How can I not give back to the earth that has so generously given to me?

Yes, each of us can make a difference in our own way! Aldo Leopold, Sigurd Olson, Bob Marshall, Olaus and Margaret Murie, Stuart Udall, Gifford Pinchot, Henry David Thoreau, Herma Baggley and millions of others have given back to the earth in their unique ways that will impact generations to come. The Aboriginal Australians have a fascinating way of stewarding the earth. Early in life, each villager is assigned a part of nature, their "Yuri," to watch and care for. One villager is responsible for the sea turtles, another for the whales, another for a certain species of bird, and so on. The stewards tune into the health of that animal. If the village is concerned about the animal or has a desire to harvest, the steward is asked to speak on behalf of the animal, with the final word on what care might be needed or whether hunting will be allowed. If the species is thriving, hunting will be allowed. If the species is in peril, hunting is denied. Rather than compelling each villager to watch over all parts of nature, the village manageably divides and focuses the care.

The more we honor and celebrate the earth, the more we become active stewards. The earth offers amazing inspiration for our creative expression. Write a poem or a song about the sky, plant a garden, photograph wild birds, hike to a mountain lake, dance around a bonfire, write in your journal beside your favorite stream or river. There are thousands of ways to express your love of nature.

The earth we live on, with its beautiful animals, flowing rivers, blossoming flowers, breathtaking sunsets, and exquisite landscapes, is precious. I feel peaceful and in awe in the presence of a mountain, gazing, wondering, and marveling at the uplift and erosion processes that have continued for millions of years.

The mountains call me to put one foot in front of the other and to hike, explore, and climb onward and upward.

The earth's abundance is remarkable. I so appreciate the gift of paper that trees so wonderfully provide, and I am committed to actions that honor the trees. I use recycled paper for all my products and participate in the 100% Replanted program by replanting ten new seedling trees for every 217 lbs. of paper I use.

There are so many great organizations that are working hard to care for the earth. It is simply a matter of choosing which ones to support. It's easy to assume that other people will keep these organizations alive, but if each of us does our small part by donating money or time, they will succeed in their work to restore healthy environments for all of us.

YourTrueNature.com has "learning links" that correspond to our Advice products. Choose your favorite tree, animal, landscape, or habitat and find out how you can help it thrive. The site also features wonderful, free Nature Curriculum for teachers and parents to encourage in children a love of the natural world. The curriculum's activities include art, writing, music, performance, celebrations, stewardship actions, and much more.

The mountains that I most remember are Pikes Peak in Colorado; the Eiger, Jungfrau, Mönch, and the Matterhorn of Switzerland; Mt. Hood in Oregon; and Mt. Ranier in Washington. I have felt their cool mountain breezes, seen their colorful meadows of wildflowers, crunched through their freshly fallen snows, leaned against their trees, and watched clouds swirl around their summits. Their majestic height invites me to reach higher in my aspirations as an active and successful steward of the earth. This is my small gift in return for such magnificence.

Living Your
True Nature

What is our purpose, and how do we find it? It's easy to become so preoccupied with making a living that we forget to really live. When we live our true nature, we are called to discover what gives meaning to our lives, to go beyond ourselves in service to others, to live in harmony with nature, to express our uniqueness, and to realize our dreams.

We can learn much from nature, especially the trees. They are perfectly content being exactly who they are. The cottonwood does not try to emulate a willow, and the redwood doesn't try to imitate an oak . . . a simple and powerful reminder that we only need to be ourselves, as the true nature of who we are is amazing and incredible. Take the time to sit under different varieties of trees so you can experience both their similarities and uniqueness. We humans have common hopes, desires, and needs, but our special mix of talents, experience, geography, and timing makes our life's path absolutely unique. Not only will the trees guide each of us to find and live our true nature, but so will the rivers, mountains, skies, animals, and plants. We simply need to slow down, release our distractions, and be open to patient listening.

The journey to finding my own life's purpose, and creating work aligned with that purpose, was not easy. A close friend helped me unravel my confusion until I arrived at the powerful answer . . . TREES. Trees give me a sense of connection, safety, inspiration, and passion. I realized that the old cottonwood tree was not something outside of me—the tree and I were one. We were both standing tall and proud, feeling the strong connection with the earth, through our roots, branching out higher, and providing shade for others. The tree was my guide and my joy.

Today, to keep myself aligned with my sense of purpose, I ask myself these ten questions: Am I living with intention and directing my life—or am I controlled by outside factors? Is there a flow to life, or does it seem like I'm swimming upriver? Am I expressing my unique gifts and talents? Am I caring for the earth and giving back in gratitude for its abundance?

Am I finding and living my joy and also serving others? Am I open to receiving the wisdom of others?

Am I living a life of trust, clarity, alignment, and peace? Am I facing life's challenges and using them to grow, change, evolve, and become? Do I question the way things are and have the courage to make things the way they could be? Am I allowing myself to be tamed— or am I keeping my wildness alive?

Living our true nature is not something we strive to achieve; rather, it's a constant path of awareness, discernment, willingness, and openness. It's a daily practice of seeing what each new day brings. When I leaned against the gnarled, ridged bark of an old tree, I asked for help. *How can I live my life with purpose and give back for this incredible gift of life I have been given? I need your help. I need your advice.* The giant tree shared its wisdom with the words for Advice from a Tree. I listened and wrote them down. One by one, I created expressions of these beautiful and timely words—a postcard, bookmark, poster, book, and journal—so I could share them with others. The feedback I got was that they touched and guided others as they had guided me. In an ever-unfolding journey, those few words from the tree were the seeds that inspired advice from over one hundred elements of nature.

To stay on track in living my true nature, I have incorporated these approaches into my life:

 Practicing meditation: taking time to sit and release, breathe, and clear.

 Journaling: a wonderful way to dialogue through words and pictures and capture the ideas that come to me. Sometimes while I'm journaling, poems flow through me.

 Clarifying intentions: concise written statements of what I intend to do or how I intend to be. I often write my intentions in my journal.

Learning: seeking out mentors who can help me answer my big questions and guide my path.

 Traveling: a chance to get away from my daily routine and take a breather. A time to ask questions and receive guidance, relax in nature, clarify my goals, and gain the perspective and clarity I need to make course corrections in my life.

These five thoughtful practices have helped me live my true nature, and to evolve and grow and support others in living their true nature.

As the mountain says, to summit all up . . .

Your True Nature

Your true and amazing nature is to rise like the sun,
to greet each day with your absolute brilliance
and shine your light for others.
Your true nature is the mountain.
To rise above it all, reach for new heights,
make solid decisions, and always be uplifting.
Your true nature is the river.
To go with the flow, stay current,
and remember that the beauty is in the journey.
Your true nature is the garden.
To plant seeds of kindness, sow seeds of happiness,
cultivate lasting friendships, take thyme for yourself,
and always dew your best.
Your true nature is the tree.
To stand tall and proud, branch
out to your full potential,
stay rooted in love, and enjoy the view!
Your true nature is to reach and grow
so that one day you can look back, and with a smile,
know you have lived your life in a way
that makes you proud.

Other friends of the mountain
share their advice . . .

Advice from a Mountain Goat

Celebrate your kidding nature

A goatee is always in style

When life gets rocky, hang on

Know when to hoof it

Show up in unexpected places

Sometimes you have to toot
your own horn

Climb to new heights!

Advice from a Glacier

Carve your own path

Go slow

Channel your strengths

Smooth the way for others

Keep moving forward

Avoid meltdowns

Be cool!

Ilan Shamir's
Advice Book Series

 Advice from a Tree &
accompanying journal

 Advice from a River &
accompanying journal

 Advice from a Mountain &
accompanying journal

 Advice from a Garden

Advice from Nature
 (Includes Advice from a Sea Turtle,
Owl, Canyon, and many more)

More Advice from Nature
(Includes Advice from a Moose,
Wildflower, Night Sky, and many more)

Other Titles

Tree Celebrations–
Planning and Celebrating Trees

PoetTree–
The Wilderness I Am

Simple Wisdom–
A Thousand Things Went Right Today!

The True Nature of Designing and
Promoting Successful Products

The True Nature of Designing and
Promoting Successful Programs

My Colorado–
Nuggets of Wit and Wisdom

Words

*We invite you to visit us at
yourtruenature.com for hundreds of other
items, including collectible and frameable
art cards, bookmarks, posters, mugs,
magnets, T-shirts and more.*

Journal Pages

Write about mountains that are special to you . . .

Earth and sky, woods
and fields, lakes and rivers,
the mountain and the sea, are
excellent schoolmasters, and
teach some of us more than we
can ever learn from books.

John Lubbock

Draw a picture of a mountain, paste photos, or write a mountain poem...

For nature activities, visit:
yourtruenature.com/activities

Ilan's Special Thanks

Laurel, my beautiful and powerful daughter, thank you for standing in your own wisdom as we walk side by side, caring for the beauty of the earth and each other. You are a special gift to me and the world.

Deep gratitude to the awesome and amazing team at Your True Nature, Inc. Special thanks to Patti, Allison, and Jill. You truly rock!

Thanks, Jasmine Quinsier, for your bringing your graphics, talents, and smiles to help package our Advice Collectibles Series. And to Kristen Barendsen for finding things that no other copy editor could possibly find. A great big thanks to you, Stella Togo, my book writing and marketing coach for your finishing touches that made this body of work come together with style.

To Tim Merriman, a master of interpretation who teaches the world about caring, connection and telling the stories that really matter.

Many thanks to you, Larry Frederick, for dedicating your career to preserving, protecting, and educating us about national parks and the many years in service as chief of interpretation for Rocky Mountain National Park.

Thank you, John Muir, for your steadfast courage and expressive words to protect Yosemite National Park and other lands that I so cherish.

Keynote programs
Breakouts
Workshops

Through the simplicity and beauty of trees and nature, Ilan Shamir calls us to branch out, grow, and celebrate our true nature! Author of the bestselling Advice from Nature products and "A Thousand Things Went Right Today," Ilan's inspiring programs are a perfect addition to conferences and events.

Member of the:
*National Association for Interpretation
*National Speakers Association Colorado
*National Storytellers Network

yourtruenature.com

Have a Tree Planted
for Someone Special!

Your purchase price of $8.95 for one tree, or $18.95 for a three-tree grove, plants and cares for native trees in projects in El Salvador, Honduras, Costa Rica, and Nicaragua through the nonprofit organization Trees, Water & People. The recipient gets a beautiful personalized greeting card from you, and both you and the recipient can visit the planting area online!

A simple gift that lasts a lifetime!
It's as easy as 1, 2, TREE . . .

Qty ($8.95)	Qty ($18.95)	Occasion
___	___	All Occasion

(Friendship, birthday, Mother's Day, thank you, birth, anniversary, congratulations, Father's Day, wedding, graduation)

___	Holiday
___	Memorial

Your Name _____

Address _____

City/State/ZIP _____

Email _____

Telephone _____

Total Qty _____ at $ 8.95 = $_____

Total Qty _____ at $18.95 = $_____

Shipping $_____ 6.50

GRAND TOTAL $_____

Send with your check to:
Your True Nature, Inc. Box 272309
Fort Collins, CO 80527, (970)282-1620
Email: orders@yourtruenature.com
Visit our website for more information or to order online at yourtruenature.com

Made in the USA
San Bernardino, CA
20 March 2017